Riddles and Brain Teasers for Intelligent Kids

333 Of The Best Brain Teasers, Trick Questions And Logic Riddles For Expanding Your Child's Mind And Supercharging Their Brain Power

Jenny Jacobs

Table of Contents

Are You Ready for Some Fun Brain Teasers?. 7

Who is This Book For?. 8

How to Use this Book?...8

55 Riddles that Will Make You Smarter 9

55 Riddles that Will Make You Giggle. 17

55 Riddles about Your Favourite Characters. 25

55 Riddles about Sports. 32

55 Riddles to Share With Your Family 39

55 Riddles to Impress Your Friends. 46

Answers to Riddles that Will Make You Smarter 53

Answers to Riddles that Will Make You Giggle. 55

Answers to Riddles about Your Favourite Characters. 57

Answers to Riddles about Sports. 59

Answers to Riddles to Share with Your Family 61

Answers to Riddles to Impress Your Friends. 63

The Best for Last. 65

Conclusion. 66

SPECIAL BONUS!

Want These 2 Bonus Books for <u>free</u>?

 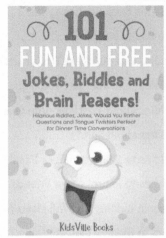

Get <u>FREE</u>, unlimited access to these and all of our new books by joining the KidsVille Books Facebook group!

SCAN W/ YOUR CAMERA TO JOIN!

PLUS! Get entered into our monthly $20 Amazon Gift card Giveaway

Are You Ready for Some Fun Brain Teasers?

All children love things that make them wonder and challenge their minds in a playful way. Not only are riddles a fun way to spend time with your child, they help in developing their reading comprehension and problem solving skills. But it does not stop there.

- Riddles are an amazing tool for improving your child's linguistic capabilities and vocabulary. When words that they might not understand come their way, they are motivated to find out what they mean in order to solve the riddle.

- Spending quality time with children and indulging in the activity of funny brain teasers is one of the very rare experiences that inculcate intellectual humor in a developing brain.

- The most difficult questions often have the simplest answers. This is a concept that changes our perception and makes us want to believe everything has a solution. Instilling such a useful value in children early on helps in them gauging the world around them with positivity and rational thinking.

Not all riddles are whacky or difficult for children but the look in their eyes when they get one right is priceless. Here is your chance to give your kids something that will boost their mood and make them harbor a good sense of accomplishment.

In 333 Riddles That Will Keep You Guessing you will find a collection of favorite and classic brain teasers. The riddles are categorized according to the theme of the moment, making it easier for kids to choose.

Who is This Book For?

This book is for kids who could use a fun challenge. Brain teasers can be more than just about context and comprehension. It is one of the simplest activities that offers multiple benefits and time well spent, whether it is between family members or friends.

The 333 riddles pique interest in young minds and help parents teach their children the value of wit and at the same time logical thinking.

How to Use this Book?

They grow up so fast. Are you sure you have all the memories? What's stopping you from adding this one to the roster as well? Quality time spent doing something productive while also filled with laughter is the kind of happiness we all seek.

Keep this book close for times that demand some fun. Long road trips, sunny picnics at the park, or waiting rooms that can make anyone annoyed and restless.

The riddles can be used to nurture creativity and strengthen resolve in children to never give up when faced with a problem.

55 Riddles that Will Make You Smarter

Riddle 1. What has a head, four legs but only one foot.

(See page 53)

Riddle 2. Can you spell cold using only two letters?

(See page 53)

Riddle 3. How many letters does the alphabet have?

(See page 53)

Riddle 4. What is at the very center of gravity?

(See page 53)

Riddle 5. There is a word in the dictionary with double letters that appear consecutively three times. What word is it?

(See page 53).

Riddle 6. What has a tail, a head, and is brown in color, but has no legs at all?

(See page 53)

Riddle 7. "The tortoise kept the taffy he took from Thomas". How many T's are in that?

(See page 53)

Riddle 8. What is the only thing that when it goes up it never comes down?

(See page 53)

Riddle 9. The more you take away, the bigger it gets. How is it possible?
(See page 53)

Riddle 10. How many items can an empty backpack hold?
(See page 53)

Riddle 11. What is heavier, a pound of cement or a pound of feathers?
(See page 53)

Riddle 12. What one word in the English language has hundreds of letters?
(See page 53)

Riddle 13. Where have you seen the cart come before the horse that pulls it?
(See page 53)

Riddle 14. You break it with the lightest squeak. What is it?
(See page 53)

Riddle 15. What has a lifespan of a few hours? The thinner it is the quicker it dies, the fatter it is the slower it dies.
(See page 53)

Riddle 16. I dance in front of your eyes, if you come too close I will eat you. What am I?
(See page 53)

Riddle 17. It was raining outside and the cat walked in, but it did not have a single damp hair. How can this be?

(See page 53)

Riddle 18. This box has no lock or key, but it has a golden treasure inside it. What is it?

(See page 53)

Riddle 19. What smells bad when it is alive, but smells good when it is dead?

(See page 53)

Riddle 20. You can rearrange this word and make it into its own past tense. What is it?

(See page 53)

Riddle 21. If a cube has a two inch length on each edge, what would its eight sides measure in square inches?

(See page 53)

Riddle 22. What happens twice in a moment, occurs once in a minute, but you will never find it in a day?

(See page 53)

Riddle 23. What is the right way to say this: "the yolk of eggs are white" or "the yolk of egg is white"?

(See page 53)

Riddle 24. A rooster lays an egg at the peak of a sloped roof. one side is the pond, on the other is the pig pen, which way will the egg fall?

(See page 53)

Riddle 25. A son and a father are in a car accident. When they are rushed to the hospital the doctor exclaims, "That is my son!" How can this be if the doctor is not lying?
(See page 53)

Riddle 26. A cowboy rides into town on Monday, he rides in again three days later on Monday. How is this possible?
(See page 53)

Riddle 27. What is the only time when a door stops being a door?
(See page 53)

Riddle 28. How do you spell rotted with only two letters?
(See page 53)

Riddle 29. I am in your words, and I touch your face, I end space and birds love me. What am I?
(See page 53)

Riddle 30. What can you catch but cannot throw?
(See page 53)

Riddle 31. The first time you see me I am yellow and in grass, the next time I am white, the third time, I fly away. What am I?
(See page 54)

Riddle 32. What never falls but always breaks?
(See page 54)

Riddle 33. What always falls but never breaks?

(See page 54)

Riddle 34. It has no mouth or voice, but it replies to you each time. What is it?

(See page 54)

Riddle 35. What has a bed but it never sleeps, has a mouth but never speaks?

(See page 54)

Riddle 36. It walks on wind, but stops when it's moist, it gnaws rocks and counts time. What is it?

(See page 54)

Riddle 37. It will keep eating and keep getting bigger. But the moment you give it water, it will die. What is it?

(See page 54)

Riddle 38. It has no sword or spear but its reign many fear. It is not a king, what is it?

(See page 54)

Riddle 39. It has two eyes with many more behind. What is it?

(See page 54)

Riddle 40. What sort of can cannot be opened with a can opener?

(See page 54)

Riddle 41. What has armour, but no weapons?
(See page 54)

Riddle 42. What peels like an onion but does not become any less?
(See page 54)

Riddle 43. When is coming across a white cat considered bad luck?
(See page 54)

Riddle 44. Its heart is as hard as stone, though when you squeeze it, it cries tears of blood. What is it?
(See page 54)

Riddle 45. Many desire it like gold, though it is not found in any vault. What is it?
(See page 54)

Riddle 46. You remove its outside, you cook the inside, then eat the outside, and throw away the inside. What is it?
(See page 54)

Riddle 47. It is never thirsty but is always drinking. It does not need air, and is found in a school. What is it?
(See page 54)

Riddle 48. I have many eyes but I live in the dark. What am I?

(See page 54)

Riddle 49. I have really short hair, and a stone in my throat. What am I?

(See page 54)

Riddle 50. I am invisible in water, and when not in it I am very valuable. Too much of me can be poison. What am I?

(See page 54)

Riddle 51. A red dungeon with many soldiers has no doors or windows. Once the soldiers leave, they make their own dungeons. What is it?

(See page 54)

Riddle 52. What has a living heart that never beats?

(See page 54)

Riddle 53. What kind of room has no space inside it for anyone?

(See page 54)

Riddle 54. What has ears but never hears anything?

(See page 54)

Riddle 55. What is the only vegetable that makes you cry when it is dead?

(See page 54)

55 Riddles that Will Make You Giggle

Riddle 1. Three eyes have the power to knock down ten soldiers. What are the three eyes?
(See page 55)

Riddle 2. This thing is right in front of you, but you fail to see it no matter how hard you try. What is it?
(See page 55)

Riddle 3. This thing is so weightless, that if you put it in a bucket of water, it will become much lighter. What is it?

(See page 55)

Riddle 4. I am beaten and burned, without that I am not yet useful. What am I?
 (See page 55)

Riddle 5. If you scratch my head I turn black. What am I?
(See page 55)

Riddle 6. You can build this house without nails, or bricks, or glue and it will house multiples. What is it?
(See page 55)

Riddle 7. It is so soft you can gouge it with your hand, but no fire can burn it. What is it?

(See page 55)

Riddle 8. What is the lightest thing on earth, but even the strongest man cannot hold it for more than a few minutes?

(See page 55)

Riddle 9. What goes up and down, but never moves?
(See page 55)

Riddle 10. You can find entire cities with roads and shops and houses, but no people live here. Where is it?

(See page 55)

Riddle 11. You bring it in when you don't need it, but throw it out when you need it. What is it?

(See page 55)

Riddle 12. There is gold hidden in every wall of this house, but no guard protects it. What is it?

(See page 55)

Riddle 13. I have a long neck, but have no head, a thousand legs but still cannot stand. What am I?

(See page 55)

Riddle 14. It just cries all the time, and does not even realise with every tear it is dying. What is it?

Riddle 15. The one who made it does not want it, the one who pays for it does not need it. What is it?

(See page 55)

Riddle 16. All I do is point and people thank me for taking them all over the world. What am I?

(See page 55)

Riddle 17. The world's most unusual book has the index coming before introduction, and the foreword coming after the epilogue, what book is it?
(See page 55)

Riddle 18. It always comes in darkness but you see it in full light. What is it?
(See page 55)

Riddle 19. The only way you can use this thing is if you break it. What is it?
(See page 55)

Riddle 20. We are twins, we never touch but still become one. What are we?
(See page 55)

Riddle 21. What has fingers and a thumb, but no blood or bone?

(See page 55)

Riddle 22. Even without a top or bottom I can easily hold flesh and blood. What am I?

(See page 55)

Riddle 23. What has hands but never claps at any of your achievements?

(See page 55)

Riddle 24. What has four legs but never walks?

(See page 55)

Riddle 25. What is common between a shark and a comb?

(See page 55)

Riddle 26. It takes so much space, the more of it there is, the harder it becomes to see anything clearly. What is it?

(See page 55)

Riddle 27. The more you add to this word the shorter it becomes. What is it?

(See page 55)

Riddle 28. It is made of gold, but also made of stone. In a deck of cards it is present 58 times. What is it?

(See page 55)

Riddle 29. What must be broken before you get to know about it?

(See page 55)

Riddle 30. I can run without legs, but I cannot walk. What am I?

(See page 55)

Riddle 31. What travels the world, but stays in one corner all the time?

(See page 56)

Riddle 32. What has a face, arms but no torso, or legs?

(See page 56)

Riddle 33. At night it has a head, in the morning it does not. What is it?

(See page 56)

Riddle 34. It has 88 working keys, but none of them open any locks. What is it?

(See page 56)

Riddle 35. What has a horn but cannot honk?

(See page 56)

Riddle 36. What sort of cup is bad at holding water?

(See page 56)

Riddle 37. What is found in Europe, but not in France Germany, Switzerland, Italy, and Spain?

(See page 56)

Riddle 38. What is hot, has a bell, but never rings?

(See page 56)

Riddle 39. Why did the crackers and buns want to go to the hospital?

(See page 56)

Riddle 40. Thomas was invited to a party on a boat. Approaching it he saw many people dancing on deck, when he entered the boat it did not have a single person onboard. How can this be?

(See page 56)

Riddle 41. No matter what you do, you can never truly answer "yes" to this question. What is it?

(See page 56)

Riddle 42. What did History say to English when they were arguing?

(See page 56)

Riddle 43. What kind of knight never eats or sleep?

(See page 56)

Riddle 44. You can crack me and I still won't be broken. What am I?

(See page 56)

Riddle 45. What is a letter that you can eat?

(See page 56)

Riddle 46. Why did the woman throw the butter out the window?
(See page 56)

Riddle 47. If you break it people applause, what is it?
(See page 56)

Riddle 48. You can harbour it, hold it, and carry it, but not with your arms. What is it?
(See page 56)

Riddle 49. It has hundreds of holes yet is considered great for security. What is it?
(See page 56)

Riddle 50. What is black and white and red all over?
(See page 56)

Riddle 51. What keeps getting damp the more it dries?
(See page 56)

Riddle 52. What is so big it could never enter your house, but people often talk about it being in a room?
(See page 56)

Riddle 53. It was never alive, but it dies. What is it?

(See page 56)

Riddle 54. What has wheels and also flies?
(See page 56)

Riddle 55. Sam's dad has 5 sons: John, Jameson, Jimmy, and Josh, what is the name of the fifth son?
(See page 56)

55 Riddles about Your Favourite Characters

Riddle 1. How did the Queen of Hearts lose her hat?

(See page 57)

Riddle 2. Why was Alice late for tea?

(See page 57)

Riddle 3. I am black and white and I am not supposed to be in Madagascar. Who am I?

(See page 57)

Riddle 4. Why did no one want Cinderella in their Football team?

(See page 57)

Riddle 5. Though many call me ruthless, I am not but my name rhymes with that word. Who am I?

(See page 57)

Riddle 6. Why was sleeping beauty waiting outside the Photo Supply Co.?

(See page 57)

Riddle 7. Why does Snow White treat all the seven dwarfs equally?

(See page 57)

Riddle 8. Where does Ariel find her missing items from her collection of things humans use?

(See page 57)

Riddle 9. Why did Jasmine want to visit the crowded marketplace?
(See page 57)

Riddle 10. What is the best kingdom in Disney?
(See page 57)

Riddle 11. Why did Elsa's parents never give her any balloons?
(See page 57)

Riddle 12. Why did Goofy build a rocket?
(See page 57)

Riddle 13. What never grows and is also an animal?
(See page 57)

Riddle 14. For someone with so many bags, I only wear one dress. Who am I?
(See page 57)

Riddle 15. Why did Tinkerbell wear a green dress?
(See page 57)

Riddle 16. You got a friend in me, who am I?
(See page 57)

Riddle 17. I am selfish but I am also helpful. I am tiny when I am supposed to be bigger. Who am I?

(See page 57)

Riddle 18. What would Ratatouille be called if it was written by Roald Dahl?

(See page 57)

Riddle 19. Why did Piglet spend hours in the toilet?

(See page 57)

Riddle 20. Why was Cinderella uncomfortable at the beach?

(See page 57)

Riddle 21. I just can't wait to be king. Who am I?

(See page 57)

Riddle 22. Why did Pocahontas gather tissues?

(See page 57)

Riddle 23. The more I take, the more I give. Who am I?

(See page 57)

Riddle 24. Why did Tramp keep standing up again and again?

(See page 57)

Riddle 25. What is the name of a princess who wishes not to be disturbed?

(See page 57)

Riddle 26. What is Donald Duck's Favourite Snack?

(See page 57)

Riddle 27. What is Snow White's least favourite dessert?

(See page 57)

Riddle 28. What did Captain Hook's first mate say to Adele?

(See page 57)

Riddle 29. Why was everyone single in Alice in Wonderland?

(See page 57)

Riddle 30. Why does Peter Pan fly so much?

(See page 57)

Riddle 31. Where did Captain Hook buy his hook from?

(See page 58)

Riddle 32. What did Daisy Duck say when she bought lipstick?

(See page 58)

Riddle 33. Why did Mickey wear an extra pair of pants to play golf?

(See page 58)

Riddle 34. Why was the Hunchback of Notre Dame made a Detective?

(See page 58)

Riddle 35. Why was Cinderella bad at acting even after weeks of practicing?

(See page 58)

Riddle 36. What prize did Gaston win that he did not appreciate?

(See page 58)

Riddle 37. Who knows the best jokes out of all the Disney Princesses?

(See page 58)

Riddle 38. What happened when Mickey and Minnie saw each other for the first time?

(See page 58)

Riddle 39. Why does Eeyore not have any friends?

(See page 58)

Riddle 40. What car did Mickey Mouse use to impress Minnie?

(See page 58)

Riddle 41. What is the Cheshire Cat's favourite milk?

(See page 58)

Riddle 42. What did Luke Skywalker get after he passed his driver's test?

(See page 58)

Riddle 43. Why did Aladdin slow down while he was being chased?

(See page 58)

Riddle 44. Why did Sleeping Beauty get in a debate with a philosopher?

(See page 58)

Riddle 45. If Dora the Explorer carried a box of puns and jokes, what would she call it?
(See page 58)

Riddle 46. Why was Bruce Wayne great at Baseball?
(See page 58

Riddle 47. Why did Superman not know he could fly as a child?
(See page 58)

Riddle 48. What does the Justice League serve in their beverages?
(See page 58)

Riddle 49. Why was Tarzan playing golf?
(See page 58)

Riddle 50. Why did the chicken cross the road?
(See page 58)

Riddle 51. Why did Mowgli live in a mud house?
(See page 58)

Riddle 52. What is Mulan's favourite part of a joke?
(See page 58)

Riddle 53. What if it doesn't scare you, no evil thing will?
(See page 58)

Riddle 54. Why did Moana answer the phone?

(See page 58)

Riddle 55. What did Bugs Bunny say to the physician who kept staring at the ceiling?

(See page 58)

55 Riddles about Sports

Riddle 1. What is a team of four bullfighters who fall into quicksand called?

(See page 59)

Riddle 2. What do you call a boomerang that does not come back?

(See page 59)

Riddle 3. What is a ghost's favourite position in soccer?

(See page 59)

Riddle 4. What is the favourite colour of a coach?

(See page 59)

Riddle 5 What do cheerleaders love to eat for breakfast?

(See page 59)

Riddle 6. Why are babies good at basketball?

(See page 59)

Riddle 7. Why did they arrest the basketball player?

(See page 59)

Riddle 8. Why do basketball players always eat donuts?

(See page 59)

Riddle 9. Why wouldn't they let the pig play basketball?

(See page 59)

Riddle 10. What is common between a good baseball team and delicious pancakes?
(See page 59)

Riddle 11. What is a golfer's favourite letter?
(See page 59)

Riddle 12. What is the best animal to play baseball with?
(See page 59)

Riddle 13. Why are baseball players so cool?
(See page 59)

Riddle 14. What sport are waiters the best at?
(See page 59)

Riddle 15 Why is badminton such a loud sport?
(See page 59)

Riddle 16. Why do football coaches go to the bank?
(See page 59)

Riddle 17. Why did the ballerina decide to quit?
(See page 59)

Riddle 18 What is an insect's favourite sport?
(See page 59)

Riddle 19. What is common between a magician and a hockey player?

(See page 59)

Riddle 20. What is the hardest part about skydiving?

(See page 59)

Riddle 21. What baseball team is great at taking care of animals?

(See page 59)

Riddle 22. What sport is famous around the world and starts with a T?

(See page 59)

Riddle 23. What basket is only useful with a hole in it?

(See page 59)

Riddle 24. What is longer: Running from first base to second, or running from second base to third?

(See page 59)

Riddle 25. What ball has limbs but cannot walk?

(See page 59)

Riddle 26. What is a butterfly's favourite sport?

(See page 59)

Riddle 27. A tomato, a cabbage, and a faucet were in a race. How do you think it went?

(See page 59)

Riddle 28. What can you play and also eat?

(See page 59)

Riddle 29. Two people who were playing chess, at the end of the game, they both had won. How is this possible?

(See page 59)

Riddle 30. What nationality never fails to complete marathon races?

(See page 59)

Riddle 31. What Bishop destroys?

(See page 60)

Riddle 32. Why are soccer players always confused?

(See page 60)

Riddle 33. You use these 5 things all the time and they are found in a tennis court. What are they?

(See page 60)

Riddle 34. Why was the pharaoh pleased with the cheerleaders?

(See page 60)

Riddle 35. It swings on sticks and shows off its tricks, uses a white powder to grip and likes applause at every flip. What is it?

(See page 60)

Riddle 36. What do boxers and fishermen have in common?

(See page 60)

Riddle 37. In what sport does the other side score without even touching the ball?

(See page 60)

Riddle 38. The score was 2-0 at the end of a football game, but no man had scored on the field. How can this be?

(See page 60)

Riddle 39. How can you make a slow athlete fast?

(See page 60)

Riddle 40. What baseball goes crazy?

(See page 60)

Riddle 41. You have this twice in swimming, three times in weightlifting, but once in tennis. What is it?

(See page 60)

Riddle 42. What do you call two people who don't like each other much and are separated by a web?

(See page 60)

Riddle 43. People always step on me with dirt, but come running to me when they are in trouble. What am I?

(See page 60)

Riddle 44. What is the hardest thing about cricket?

(See page 60)

Riddle 45. What sport is a French Christian's favourite?

(See page 60)

Riddle 46. If a knife had a baby with a shoe, what would they call it?

(See page 60)

Riddle 47. Why do waiters hate volleyball?

(See page 60)

Riddle 48. Why do thieves prefer baseball?

(See page 60)

Riddle 49. Why do lawyers love tennis?

(See page 60)

Riddle 50. What did the goalie say to the ball
they miss?

(See page 60)

Riddle 51. James is a soccer player, every time he touches the ball with his hands he is not given a penalty. Why?

(See page 60)

Riddle 52. What sport do chatterboxes wish they could enjoy all the time?

(See page 60)

Riddle 53. What does Santa Claus use for skiing?

(See page 60)

Riddle 54. What beverage do Hockey players dislike?

) (See page 60

Riddle 55. What basketball team does Santa Claus cheer for?

(See page 60)

55 Riddles to Share With Your Family

Riddle 1. What is present at the start of an eternity, and at the end of time and space?

(See page 61)

Riddle 2. What is common between a bell and an orange?

(See page 61

Riddle 3. What is on its way all the time but never arrives?

(See page 61)

Riddle 4. This cannot run without winding at some point. What is it?

(See page 61

Riddle 5. What is yours but other people keep using it?

(See page 61)

Riddle 6. What is common between a person in love and a welder?

(See page 61)

Riddle 7. At what time is a watch like a train?

(See page 61)

Riddle 8. What has more trees than the forest?

(See page 61)

Riddle 9. How many sides does a sphere have?

(See page 61)

Riddle 10. What has branches, but no leaves, or bark?

(See page 61)

Riddle 11. What is the thing that no one wants to have, but no one wants to lose either?

(See page 61)

Riddle 12. Which president wore the largest hat?

(See page 61)

Riddle 13. The men on a boat have cigarettes but no lighter, how do they light a cigarette?

(See page 61)

Riddle 14. What is common between a piece of wood and a person?

(See page 61)

Riddle 15. What travels on four in the morning, two at noon, and four again at the end of the day?

(See page 61)

Riddle 16. What nationality is always in a hurry?

(See page 61)

Riddle 17. What is Joan of Arc made of?

(See page 61)

Riddle 18. When is a fight like a pretty woman?
(See page 61)

Riddle 19. What is common between grass and silk?
(See page 61)

Riddle 20 What men are always above board?
(See page 61)

Riddle 21. No matter how much you throw it away, it never leaves you. What is it?
(See page 61)

Riddle 22. What kind of pins do you find in a soup?
(See page 61)

Riddle 23. How is a bandstand and an oven the same for a musician?
(See page 61)

Riddle 24. When is a mountain top like a bank account?
(See page 61)

Riddle 25. When do painters use triggers and not brushes?
(See page 61)

Riddle 28. Where does success come before work?

40

(See page 61)

Riddle 27. What is the capital of France?
(See page 61)

Riddle 28. I am found in Mercury, Earth, Mars, Jupiter, and Uranus, but not in Venus or Neptune.
What am I?
(See page 61)

Riddle 29. I make a lot of noise when I am changing, when I am done, I weigh much lighter. What am I?
(See page 61)

Riddle 30. A bus driver was going the wrong way on a one-way street, yet no one thought this was wrong, why?
(See page 61)

Riddle 31. I can fill up spaces entirely and still not take up any room. What am I?
(See page 62)

Riddle 32. Even though sharing is encouraged, this is the only thing that is frowned upon when you share it. What is it?
(See page 62)

Riddle 33. There is a rail track without any trains. How can you spell that without R?

(See page 62)

Riddle 34. What can jump higher than a building?
(See page 62)

Riddle 35. What do bunnies dance to?
(See page 62)

Riddle 36. Where do sick boats go?
(See page 62)

Riddle 37. You have no use for it, and it is a very boring companion. You can't lose it if you tried. What is it?
(See page 62)

Riddle 38. I sound like a parrot, but I am orange with a green hat. What am I?
(See page 62)

Riddle 39. What is the saddest fruit?
(See page 62)

Riddle 40. A monkey in Asia is called Lulu, a monkey in Africa is called Lala. What is a monkey in Antarctica called?
(See page 62)

Riddle 41. What has a bottom at the very top?
(See page 62)

Riddle 42. What food's house must you throw away before you can eat it?
(See page 62)

Riddle 43. What do clouds wear underneath their raincoats?
(See page 62)

Riddle 44. Why do ducks need tail feathers?
(See page 62)

Riddle 45. Where do cows spend their weekends?
(See page 62)

Riddle 46. What tire does not move when you turn the car to the left?
(See page 62)

Riddle 47. Why does the moon refuse to eat once a month?
(See page 62)

Riddle 48. What has hundreds of needles but does not know how to sew?
(See page 62)

Riddle 49. Where do fish store their treasure?
(See page 62)

Riddle 50. Why are monkeys so fit?
(See page 62)

Riddle 51. What invention can let you see through a wall?

(See page 62)

Riddle 52. What is a toad's favourite game?
(See page 62)

Riddle 53. What do cheerleaders like to drink?
(See page 62)

Riddle 54. What ball can you roll but cannot hold or throw?
(See page 62)

Riddle 55. I am made of trees, lifted by the breeze, I like to hang in the sky, though I am connected to the ground. What am I?
(See page 62)

55 Riddles to Impress Your Friends

Riddle 1. Why should you not tell a joke when you are ice skating?
(See page 63)

Riddle 2. Why was the mummy not invited to the Halloween party?
(See page 63)

Riddle 3. What is common between lollipops and racehorses?
(See page 63)

Riddle 4. How can you jump over three men without even getting up?
(See page 63)

Riddle 5. This becomes harder to catch the faster you run. What is it?
(See page 63)

Riddle 6. Why did the man do the backstroke?
(See page 63)

Riddle 7. How do fireflies start a marathon?
(See page 63)

Riddle 8. A dog was tied to a 6 foot leash, but he managed to run 15 feet. How is this possible?
(See page 63)

Riddle 9. What is a sheep that does karate?

(See page 63)

Riddle 10. Why did the banker take down the trampoline?
(See page 63)

Riddle 11. What is the best exercise for losing weight?
(See page 63)

Riddle 12. What should you do if you are swimming in the ocean and an alligator attacks you?
(See page 63)

Riddle 13. What did one fish say to the other fish?
(See page 63)

Riddle 14. Two men were racing on the beach, the winner won despite the sand in his shoe. How?
(See page 63)

Riddle 15. What sort of cats like bowling?
(See page 63)

Riddle 16. Why did they make the elephants leave the swimming pool?
(See page 63)
Riddle 17. Why do they say that Adam was a great runner?
(See page 63)

Riddle 18. What has 18 legs and is good at catching flies?

(See page 63)

Riddle 19. Why are mountain climbers the most curious people in the world?

(See page 63)

Riddle 20. Why did they hire the piano tuner to play baseball?

(See page 63)

Riddle 21. I am heavy, I have 7 letters. If you take 2 letters away I become 8, if you take 1 letter away I become 80. What am I?

(See page 63)

Riddle 22. A man travelled the world in a ship, though everywhere he went land was always in sight. How come?

(See page 63)

Riddle 23. John was 25 years old when he died of old age. How is this possible?

(See page 63)

Riddle 24. What do skeletons like to eat?

(See page 63)

Riddle 25. I am named after the animal I eat. What am I?

(See page 63)

Riddle 26. You walk into a room with a rabbit, a bear, and a monkey. What is the smartest animal in the room?

(See page 63)

Riddle 27. I am surrounded by wood but I come from a mine. What am I?

(See page 63)

Riddle 28. The place I belong to also belongs to me. What is it?

(See page 63)

Riddle 29. I start with M and end with X but have different letters every day. What am I?

(See page 63)

Riddle 30. What used to be full of thoughts but is empty now?

(See page 63)

Riddle 31. If you take off my skin I won't cry, but you will. What am I?

(See page 64)

Riddle 32. What is the least spoken language in the world?

(See page 64)

Riddle 33. What begins when a thing ends?

(See page 64)

Riddle 34. What likes to sit on a throne but is also good at measuring things?

(See page 64)

Riddle 35. What runs around town all day but never gets tired?

(See page 64)

Riddle 36. What is at the back of a cow and in front of a woman?

(See page 64)

Riddle 37. What is a snowman in summer called?

(See page 64)

Riddle 38. A rabbit breeds every month and can deliver 7 baby rabbits. If you bought a rabbit, how many baby rabbits would you have in 12 months?

(See page 64)

Riddle 39. Tom is 6 ft tall and works at a butcher shop. He also wears size 12 shoes. What does he weigh?

(See page 64)

Riddle 40. Who is never hungry at Thanksgiving?

(See page 64)

Riddle 41. The dirtier I get the whiter I become. What am I?

(See page 64)

Riddle 42. What comes from water but when it returns to it, it dies?

(See page 64)

Riddle 43. The wind is blowing at 12mph at an apple tree. What direction will the apples fall in?

(See page 64)

Riddle 44. Money cannot buy me. I am priceless to two people, but worthless when in the possession of one. What am I?

(See page 64)

Riddle 45. What is the softest nut in the world?

(See page 64)

Riddle 46. What would you call a fly without wings?

(See page 64)

Riddle 47. Why did Emily put wheels on her rocking chair?

(See page 64)

Riddle 48. What never gets wetter when it rains?

(See page 64)

Riddle 49. What do math teachers like to eat for dessert?

(See page 64)

50. Why did the coffee rush to the police station?

(See page 64)

Riddle 51. What goes off but never leaves its position?

(See page 64)

Riddle 52. What side of a house cat has the most fur?

(See page 64)

Riddle 53. Your parents have a child, it is not your brother, nor your sister, who is it?

(See page 64)

Riddle 54. What is the safest room to be in during the zombie apocalypse?

(See page 64)

Riddle 55. What do Snowmen like for breakfast?

(See page 64)

Answers to Riddles that Will Make You Smarter

1. A bed
2. IC (icy)
3. Alphabet spells out to 11 letters
4. The letter V
5. Bookkeeper
6. A penny
7. There are only 2 Ts in that
8. Your age
9. You are describing a hole
10. Only one, after that it is no longer an empty backpack
11. Both are the same.
12. Mailbox
13. In a dictionary
14. Silence
15. A candle
16. Fire
17. The cat was bald
18. An egg
19. Bacon
20. The word 'eat'
21. A cube only has six sides
22. The letter M
23. Both are wrong since yolks are yellow
24. Roosters don't lay eggs
25. The doctor is the mother of the boy
26. Monday is the horse
27. When it is ajar
28. DK (decay)
29. Air
30. The common cold
31. A dandelion

32. Dawn

33. Dusk

34. An echo

35. A river

36. Sand

37. Fire

38. Queen bee

39. A peacock

40. A pelican

41. A turtle

42. A snake

43. When you are a mouse

44. A cherry

45. Chocolate

46. Corn

47. A fish

48. A potato

49. A peach

50. Salt

51. A watermelon

52. An artichoke

53. A mushroom

54. Corn

55. An onion

Answers to Riddles that Will Make You Giggle

1. A bowling ball
2. Your future
3. A hole
4. Iron ore
5. A matchstick
6. A nest
7. A body of water
8. Breath
9. Stairs
10. A map
11. An anchor
12. A beehive
13. A broom
14. A candle
15. A coffin
16. A compass
17. A dictionary
18. Dream
19. An egg
20. Eyes
21. A glove
22. A ring
23. A clock
24. A chair
25. The first thing you look at is the teeth
26. Darkness
27. Short
28. A heart
29. News
30. A nose
31. A stamp

32. A clock

33. A pillow

34. A piano

35. A rhinoceros

36. A hiccup

37. The letter U

38. A chili pepper

39. They felt crummy

40. There were only couples at the party

41. "Are you dead?"

42. "I won't repeat myself"

43. A chess knight

44. A joke

45. A pea

46. She wanted to see butterfly

47. Record

48. A grudge

49. A chain

50. A newspaper- it is read all over

51. A towel

52. An elephant

53. Battery

54. A garbage truck

55. Sam

Answers to Riddles about Your Favourite Characters

1. It was off with her head
2. Because she fell down the rabbit hole
3. Penguin
4. Because she ran from the ball
5. Toothless
6. She was waiting for her prints to come
7. Because she is the fairest of them all
8. The Lost and Flounder box
9. She was looking for a date
10. Under the Sea- according to Sebastian it is better
11. Because they knew she would let it go
12. He wanted to visit Pluto
13. Peter Pan
14. Jane from Tarzan
15. Because she was green with envy when Peter made friends with Wendy
16. Woody
17. Mushu
18. James and the Giant Quiche
19. He was looking for Pooh
20. Because she was wearing glass flippers
21. Simba
22. Because she was going to visit the Weeping WIllow
23. Robin Hood
24. Because he was in the presence of Lady
25. Slapping beauty
26. Quacker Oats
27. Apple pie
28. "Hello. It's Smee"
29. Because there could only be one queen of hearts
30. Because he neverlands
31. The second hand store

32. "Put it on my bill"

33. In case he got a hole in one

34. He always had a hunch

35. She had a pumpkin for a coach

36. The No-Belle prize

37. Ra"puns"ell

38. It was glove at first sight

39. Because he plays with pooh all day

40. A minnie-van

41. Evaporated milk

42. A toy yoda

43. Because his enemies were ja-far

44. Because she kept singing "I wonder"

45. Pundora's Box

46. Because he was Batman

47. He didn't know his cape-abilities

48. Just ice

49. He was perfecting his swing

50. To get away from the sky that was falling

51. Because he was taught to appreciate the simple bare necessities

52. The 'punch' line

53. Cruella De Vil

54. Because the sea was calling her

55. "What's up doc?"

Answers to Riddles about Sports

1. Quatro Sinko
2. A stick
3. Ghoul Keeper
4. Yeller
5. Cheerios
6. Because they dribble
7. Because he shot the ball
8. So they can dunk them
9. Because it was a ball hog
10. They both need a good batter
11. Tee
12. A bat
13. They sit next to the fans
14. Tennis, because they have to serve the ball
15. Because the players raise a racquet
16. To get their quarter back
17. She was tu-tu scared
18. Cricket
19. They both accomplish hat tricks
20. The ground
21. The New York Vets
22. Golf
23. The basket of basketball
24. Second to third base, because there is a shortstop
25. A football
26. Swimming
27. The faucet was running, the cabbage was ahead, and the tomato tried to ketchup
28. Squash
29. They were playing against different people
30. The Finnish
31. The one on the chessboard

32. Because they have opposing goals.

33. The vowels a,e,i,o,u are present in 'a tennis court'

34. Because they made a pyramid

35. A gymnast

36. They throw hooks

37. Baseball

38. It was a women's game

39. Keep them from eating

40. A screwball

41. The letter i

42. Tennis players

43. A baseball base

44. The bat

45. Le Cross (lacrosse)

46. Ice Skate

47. Because every time they serve, it is immediately returned to them

48. Because they are rewarded for stealing bases

49. They love being in the court

50. "Catch you later"

51. James is the goalie

52. Kayakking

53. The North Pole

54. Penaltea

55. New York Old St. Knicks

Answers to Riddles to Share with Your Family

1. The letter E
2. They both need to be peeled
3. Tomorrow
4. A river
5. Your name
6. They both carry a torch
7. When it is two to two
8. A library
9. Two sides: the inside and outside
10. A bank
11. A lawsuit
12. The one with the largest head
13. They threw one cigarette overboard and made the boat a cigarette lighter
14. Both can be rulers
15. A man with a 9 to 5 job and a car
16. Russians
17. Maid of Orleans
18. When it is a knockout
19. They are both measured by the yard
20. Chessmen
21. A boomerang
22. Terrapins
23. They both help him make bread
24. When its peaks your interest
25. When they are a stick up artist
26. In the dictionary
27. The letter F
28. The letter R
29. Popcorn
30. He was walking not driving
31. Light

32. A secret

33. T-h-a-t

34. Everything that jumps, because buildings don't jump at all.

35. Hip hop music

36. To the dock

37. A shadow

38. A carrot

39. A blueberry

40. Lost

41. Your legs

42. An egg

43. Thunderwear

44. To cover their buttquacks

45. They go to the moo-vies

46. The spare tire

47. Because it is full

48. A porcupine

49. In the riverbank

50. They go to the jungle gym

51. A window

52. Leap frog

53. Root beer

54. An eyeball

55. A kite

Answers to Riddles to Impress Your Friends

1. Because the ice might crack up
2. Because they wrap things up
3. The more you lick them the faster they go
4. You are playing checkers
5. Your breath
6. He just ate and did not want to swim on a full stomach
7. Someone shouts, "ready, set, glow"
8. The leash was not tied to anything
9. A lamb chop
10. All the cheques were bouncing
11. Pushing yourself away from the table
12. Nothing, alligators don't swim in oceans
13. "If you keep your big mouth shut you won't get caught"
14. It was quicksand
15. Alley cats
16. Because they couldn't hold up their trunks
17. Because he was the first in the human race
18. A baseball team
19. They always want to take another peak
20. Because he had perfect pitch
21. Weighty
22. He was in a spaceship
23. John was born in a leap year
24. Spare ribs
25. Anteater
26. You
27. A pencil
28. Home
29. A mailbox
30. A skull
31. An onion

32. Sign language

33. Death

34. A ruler

35. Roads

36. W

37. Water

38. Zero. It takes two rabbits to breed

39. He weighs meat at the butcher's shop

40. The stuffed turkey

41. Blackboard

42. An ice cube

43. Down

44. Love

45. A donut

46. A walk

47. She liked to rock and roll

48. Water

49. Pi

50. It was mugged

51. An alarm clock

52. The outside

53. It's you

54. The living room

55. Snowflakes

The Best for Last

Did you think the fun was over? think again!

Riddle 1. You cannot keep me without giving me to someone else. What am I?

Riddle 2. I am a seed with three letters. If you take away two it doesn't matter. What am

I?

Riddle 3. When can you take away the whole, and some still remains?

Answers to the Riddles

1. Your word
2. A pea
3. When it is wholesome

Conclusion

Riddles have always delivered the best of both structural thinking as well as humor.

If you enjoyed 333 Riddles That Will Keep You Guessing, spread the word. We love it when we discover someone had a great time with the brain teasers we put together, so do not hesitate to leave a review.

If we made your day, carry it forward and make someone else's by recommending our book.

Made in the USA
Monee, IL
11 December 2020

52392819R00038